On The American Contribution

*AN ESSAY ON THE AMERICAN CONTRIBUTION AND
THE DEMOCRATIC IDEA*

Winston Churchill

1ˢᵗ WORLD
LIBRARY
Literary Society

On The American Contribution

Winston Churchill

© 1st World Library – Literary Society, 2004
PO Box 2211
Fairfield, IA 52556
www.1stworldlibrary.org
First Edition

LCCN: 2003099810

ISBN: 1-59540-133-4

Purchase *"On The American Contribution"*
as a traditional bound book at:
www.1stWorldLibrary.org/purchase.asp?ISBN=1-59540-133-4

On The American Contribution
contributed by Ed, Tim & Rodney
in support of
1st World Library - Literary Society

I

Failure to recognize that the American, is at heart an idealist is to lack understanding of our national character. Two of our greatest interpreters proclaimed it, Emerson and William James. In a recent address at the Paris Sorbonne on "American Idealism," M. Firmin Roz observed that a people is rarely justly estimated by its contemporaries. The French, he says, have been celebrated chiefly for the skill of their chefs and their vaudeville actors, while in the disturbed 'speculum mundi' Americans have appeared as a collection of money grabbers whose philosophy is the dollar. It remained for the war to reveal the true nature of both peoples. The American colonists, M. Roz continues, unlike other colonists, were animated not by material motives, but by the desire to safeguard and realize an ideal; our inherent characteristic today is a belief in the virtue and power of ideas, of a national, indeed, of a universal, mission. In the Eighteenth Century we proposed a Philosophy and adopted a Constitution far in advance of the political practice of the day, and set up a government of which Europe predicted the early downfall. Nevertheless, thanks partly to good fortune, and to the farseeing wisdom of our early statesmen who perceived that the success of our experiment depended upon the maintenance of an isolation from European affairs, we established democracy as a practical form of government.

We have not always lived up to our beliefs in ideas. In our dealings with other nations, we yielded often to imperialistic ambitions and thus, to a certain extent, justified the cynicism of Europe. We took what we wanted - and more. From Spain we seized western Florida; the annexation of Texas and the subsequent war with Mexico are acts upon which we cannot look back with unmixed democratic pride; while more than once we professed a naive willingness to fight England in order to push our boundaries further north. We regarded the Monroe Doctrine as altruistic, while others smiled. But it suited England, and her sea power gave it force.

Our war with Spain in 1898, however, was fought for an idea, and, despite the imperialistic impulse that followed it, marks a transition, an advance, in international ethics. Imperialistic cynics were not lacking to scoff at our protestation that we were fighting Spain in order to liberate Cuba; and yet this, for the American people at large, was undoubtedly the inspiration of the war. We kept our promise, we did not annex Cuba, we introduced into international affairs what is known as the Big Brother idea. Then came the Platt Amendment. Cuba was free, but she must not wallow near our shores in an unhygienic state, or borrow money without our consent. We acquired valuable naval bases. Moreover, the sudden and unexpected acquisition of Porto Rico and the Philippines made us imperialists in spite of ourselves.

Nations as well as individuals, however, must be judged by their intentions. The sound public opinion of our people has undoubtedly remained in favour of ultimate self-government for the Philippines, and the greatest measure of self-determination for little Porto

Rico; it has been unquestionably opposed to commercial exploitation of the islands, desirous of yielding to these peoples the fruits of their labour in developing the resources of their own lands. An intention, by the way, diametrically different from that of Germany. In regard to our protectorate in the island of San Domingo, our "semi-protectorate" in Nicaragua, the same argument of intention may fairly be urged. Germany, who desired them, would have exploited them. To a certain extent, no doubt, as a result of the momentum of commercial imperialism, we are still exploiting them. But the attitude of the majority of Americans toward more backward peoples is not cynical; hence there is hope that a democratic solution of the Caribbean and Central American problem may be found. And we are not ready, as yet, to accept without further experiment the dogma that tropical and sub-tropical people will not ultimately be able to govern themselves. If this eventually, prove to be the case at least some such experiment as the new British Labour Party has proposed for the Empire may be tried. Our general theory that the exploitation of foreign peoples reacts unfavourably on the exploiters is undoubtedly sound.

Nor are the ethics of the manner of our acquisition of a part of Panama and the Canal wholly defensible from the point of view of international democracy. Yet it must be remembered that President Roosevelt was dealing with a corrupt, irresponsible, and hostile government, and that the Canal had become a necessity not only for our own development, but for that of the civilization of the world.

The Spanish War, as has been said, marked a transition, a development of the American Idea. In obedience to a growing perception that dominion and exploitation are incompatible with and detrimental to our system of government, we fought in good faith to gain self-determination for an alien people. The only real peril confronting democracy is the arrest of growth. Its true conquests are in the realms of ideas, and hence it calls for a statesmanship which, while not breaking with the past, while taking into account the inherent nature of a people, is able to deal creatively with new situations - always under the guidance of current social science.

Woodrow Wilson's Mexican policy, being a projection of the American Idea to foreign affairs, a step toward international democracy, marks the beginning of a new era. Though not wholly understood, though opposed by a powerful minority of our citizens, it stirred the consciousness of a national mission to which our people are invariably ready to respond. Since it was essentially experimental, and therefore not lacking in mistakes, there was ample opportunity for a criticism that seemed at times extremely plausible. The old and tried method of dealing with such anarchy as existed across our southern border was made to seem the safe one; while the new, because it was untried, was presented as disastrous. In reality, the reverse was the case.

Mr. Wilson's opponents were, generally speaking, the commercial classes in the community, whose environment and training led them to demand a foreign policy similar to that of other great powers, a financial imperialism which is the logical counterpart in foreign affairs of the commercial exploitation of domestic national resources and domestic labour. These were the classes which combated the growth of democracy at home, in national and state politics. From their point of view - not that of the larger vision - they were consistent. On the other hand, the nation grasped the fact that to have one brand of democracy at home and another for dealing with foreign nations was not only illogical but, in the long run, would be suicidal to the Republic. And the people at large were committed to democratic progress at home. They were struggling for it.

One of the most important issues of the American liberal movement early in this century had been that for the conservation of what remains of our natural resources of coal and metals and oil and timber and waterpower for the benefit of all the people, on the theory that these are the property of the people. But if the natural resources of this country belong to the people of the United States, those of Mexico belong to the people of Mexico. It makes no difference how "lazy," ignorant, and indifferent to their own interests the Mexicans at present may be. And even more important in these liberal campaigns was the issue of the conservation of human resources - men and women and children who are forced by necessity to labour. These must be protected in health, given economic freedom and a just reward for their toil. The American democracy, committed to the principle of the conservation of domestic natural and human resources, could not without detriment to itself persist in a foreign policy that ignored them. For many years our own government had permitted the squandering of these resources by adventurous capitalists; and gradually, as we became a rich industrial nation, these capitalists sought profitable investments for their increasing surplus in foreign lands. Their manner of acquiring "concessions" in Mexico was quite similar to that by which they had seized because of the indifference and ignorance of our own people - our own mines and timber lands which our government held in trust. Sometimes these American "concessions" have been valid in law though the law itself violated a democratic principle; more often corrupt officials winked at violations of the law, enabling capitalists to absorb bogus claims.

The various rulers of Mexico sold to American and other foreign capitalists the resources belonging to the people of their country, and pocketed, with their followers, the proceeds of the sale. Their control of the country rested upon force; the stability of the Diaz rule, for instance, depended upon the "President's" ability to maintain his dictatorship - a precarious guarantee to the titles he had given. Hence the premium on revolutions. There was always the incentive to the upstart political and military buccaneer to overthrow the dictator and gain possession of the spoils, to sell new doubtful concessions and levy new tribute on the capitalists holding claims from a former tyrant.

The foreign capitalists appealed to their governments; commercial imperialism responded by dispatching military forces to protect the lives and "property" of its citizens, in some instances going so far as to take possession of the country. A classic case, as cited by Hobson, is Britain's South African War, in which the blood and treasure of the people of the United Kingdom were expended because British capitalists had found the Boers recalcitrant, bent on retaining their own country for themselves. To be sure, South Africa, like Mexico is rich in resources for which advancing civilization continually makes demands. And, in the case of Mexico, the products of the tropics, such as rubber, are increasingly necessary to the industrial powers of the temperate zone. On the other hand, if the exploiting nation aspire to self-government, the imperialistic method of obtaining these products by the selfish exploitation of the natural and human resources of the backward countries reacts so powerfully on the growth of democracy at home - and hence on the growth of democracy throughout the world - as to threaten the very future of civilization. The British Liberals, when they came into power, perceived this, and at once did their best to make amends to South Africa by granting her autonomy and virtual independence, linking her to Britain by the silken thread of Anglo-Saxon democratic culture. How strong this thread has proved is shown by the action of those of Dutch blood in the Dominion during the present war.

Eventually, if democracy is not to perish from the face of the earth, some other than the crude imperialistic method of dealing with backward peoples, of obtaining for civilization the needed resources of their lands, must be inaugurated - a democratic method. And this is perhaps the supreme problem of democracy today. It demands for its solution a complete reversal of the established policy of imperialism, a new theory of international relationships, a mutual helpfulness and partnership between nations, even as democracy implies cooperation between individual citizens. Therefore President Wilson laid down the doctrine that American citizens enter Mexico at their own risk; that they must not expert that American blood will be shed or the nation's money be expended to protect their lives or the "property" they have acquired from Mexican dictators. This applies also to the small capitalists, the owners of the coffee plantations, as well as to those Americans in Mexico who are not capitalists but wage earners. The people of Mexico are entitled to try the experiment of self-determination. It is an experiment, we frankly acknowledge that fact, a democratic experiment dependent on physical science, social science, and scientific education. The other horn of the dilemma, our persistence in imperialism, is even worse - since by such persistence we destroy ourselves.

A subjective judgment, in accordance with our own democratic standards, by the American Government as to the methods employed by a Huerta, for instance, is indeed demanded; not on the ground, however, that such methods are "good" or "bad"; but whether they are detrimental to Mexican self-determination, and hence to the progress of our own democracy.

II

If America had started to prepare when Belgium was invaded, had entered the war when the Lusitania was sunk, Germany might by now have been defeated, hundreds of thousands of lives might have been spared. All this may be admitted. Yet, looking backward, it is easy to read the reason for our hesitancy in our national character and traditions. We were pacifists, yes, but pacifists of a peculiar kind. One of our greatest American prophets, William James, knew that there was an issue for which we were ready to fight, for which we were willing to make the extreme sacrifice, - and that issue he defined as "war against war." It remained for America to make the issue.

Peoples do not rush to arms unless their national existence is threatened. It is what may be called the environmental cause that drives nations quickly into war. It drove the Entente nations into war, though incidentally they were struggling for certain democratic institutions, for international justice. But in the case of America, the environmental cause was absent. Whether or not our national existence was or is actually threatened, the average American does not believe that it is. He was called upon to abandon his tradition, to mingle in a European conflict, to fight for an idea alone. Ideas require time to develop, to seize the imagination of masses. And it must be remembered that in 1914 the great issue had not been defined. Curiously enough, now that it is defined, it proves to be an American issue - a logical and positive projection of our Washingtonian tradition and Monroe doctrine. These had for their object the preservation and development of democracy, the banishment from the Western Hemisphere of European imperialistic conflict and war. We are now, with the help of our allies, striving to banish these things from the face of the earth. It is undoubtedly the greatest idea for which man has been summoned to make the supreme sacrifice.

Its evolution has been traced. Democracy was the issue in the Spanish War, when we fought a weak nation. We have followed its broader application to Mexico, when we were willing to ignore the taunts and insults of another weak nation, even the loss of "prestige," for the sake of the larger good. And we have now the clue to the President's interpretation of the nation's mind during the first three years of the present war. We were willing to bear the taunts and insults of Germany so long as it appeared that a future world peace night best be brought about by the preservation of neutrality, by turning the weight of the impartial public opinion of our democracy and that of other neutrals against militarism and imperialism. Our national aim was ever consistent with the ideal of William James, to advance democracy and put an end to the evil of war.

The only sufficient reason for the abandonment of the Washingtonian policy is the furtherance of the object for which it was inaugurated, the advance of democracy. And we had established the precedent, with Spain and Mexico, that the Republic shall engage in no war of imperialistic conquest. We war only in behalf of, or in defence of, democracy.

Before the entrance of America, however, the issues of the European War were by no means clear cut along democratic lines. What kind of democracy were the allies fighting for? Nowhere and at no time had it been defined by any of their statesmen. On the contrary, the various allied governments had entered into compacts for the transference of territory in the event of victory; and had even, by the offer of rewards, sought to play one small nation against another. This secret diplomacy of bargains, of course, was a European heritage, the result of an imperialistic environment which the American did not understand, and from which he was happily free. Its effect on France is peculiarly enlightening. The hostility of European governments, due to their fear of her republican institutions, retarded her democratic growth, and her history during the reign of Napoleon III is one of intrigue for aggrandizement differing from Bismarck's only in the fact that it was unsuccessful. Britain, because she was separated from the continent and protected by her fleet, virtually withdrew from European affairs in the latter part of the nineteenth century, and, as a result, made great strides in democracy. The aggressions of Germany forced Britain in self-defence into coalitions. Because of her power and wealth she became the Entente leader, yet her liberal government was compelled to enter into secret agreements with certain allied governments in order to satisfy what they deemed to be their needs and just ambitions. She had honestly sought, before the war, to come to terms with Germany, and had even proposed gradual disarmament. But, despite the best intentions, circumstances and environment, as well as the precarious situation of her empire, prevented her from liberalizing her foreign relations to conform with the growth of democracy within the United Kingdom and the Dominions. Americans felt a profound pity for Belgium. But she was not, as Cuba had been, our affair. The great majority of our citizens sympathized with the Entente, regarded with amazement and disgust the sudden disclosure of the true character of the German militaristic government. Yet for the average American the war wore the complexion of other European conflicts, was one involving a Balance of Power, mysterious and inexplicable. To him the underlying issue was not democratic, but imperialistic; and this was partly because he was unable to make a mental connection between a European war and the brand of democracy he recognized. Preaching and propaganda fail unless it can be brought home to a people that something dear to their innermost nature is at stake, that the fate of the thing they most desire, and are willing to make sacrifices for, hangs in the balance.

During a decade the old political parties, between which there was now little more than an artificial alignment, had been breaking up. Americans were absorbed in the great liberal movement begun under the leadership of President Roosevelt, the result of which was to transform democracy from a static to a pragmatic and evolutionary conception, - in order to meet and correct new and unforeseen evils. Political freedom was seen to be of little worth unless also accompanied by the economic freedom the nation had enjoyed before the advent of industrialism. Clerks and farmers, professional men and shopkeepers and artisans were ready to follow the liberal leaders in states and nation; intellectual elements from colleges and universities were enlisted. Paralleling the movement, at times mingling with it, was the revolt of labour, manifested not only in political action, but in strikes and violence. Readily accessible books and magazines together with club and forum lectures in cities, towns, and villages were rapidly educating the population in social science, and the result was a growing independent vote to make politicians despair.

Here was an instance of a democratic culture growing in isolation, resentful of all external interference. To millions of Americans - especially in our middle western and western states - bent upon social reforms, the European War appeared as an arresting influence. American participation meant the triumph of the forces of reaction. Colour was lent to this belief because the conservative element which had opposed social reforms was loudest in its demand for intervention. The wealthy and travelled classes organized preparedness parades and distributed propaganda. In short, those who had apparently done their utmost to oppose democracy at home were most insistent that we should embark upon a war for democracy across the seas. Again, what kind of democracy? Obviously a status quo, commercially imperialistic democracy, which the awakening liberal was bent upon abolishing.

There is undoubtedly in such an office as the American presidency some virtue which, in times of crisis, inspires in capable men an intellectual and moral growth proportional to developing events. Lincoln, our most striking example, grew more between 1861 and 1865 than during all the earlier years of his life. Nor is the growth of democratic leaders, when seen through the distorted passions of their day, apparently a consistent thing. Greatness, near at hand, is startlingly like inconsistency; it seems at moments to vacillate, to turn back upon and deny itself, and thus lays itself open to seemingly plausible criticism by politicians and time servers and all who cry out for precedent. Yet it is an interesting and encouraging fact that the faith of democratic peoples goes out, and goes out alone, to leaders who - whatever their minor faults and failings - do not fear to reverse themselves when occasion demands; to enunciate new doctrines, seemingly in contradiction to former assertions, to meet new crises. When a democratic leader who has given evidence of greatness ceases to develop new ideas, he loses the public confidence. He flops back into the ranks of the conservative he formerly opposed, who catch up with him only when he ceases to grow.

In 1916 the majority of the American people elected Mr. Wilson in the belief that he would keep them out of war. In 1917 he entered the war with the nation behind him. A recalcitrant Middle West was the first to fill its quota of volunteers, and we witnessed the extraordinary spectacle of the endorsement of conscription: What had happened? A very simple, but a very great thing Mr. Wilson had made the issue of the war a democratic issue, an American issue, in harmony with our national hopes and traditions. But why could not this issue have been announced in 1914 or 1915? The answer seems to be that peoples, as well as their leaders and interpreters, must grow to meet critical situations. In 1861 the, moral idea of the Civil War was obscured and hidden by economic and material interests. The Abraham Lincoln who entered the White House in 1881 was indeed the name man who signed the Emancipation Proclamation in 1863; and yet, in a sense, he was not the same man; events and responsibilities had effected a profound but logical growth in his personality. And the people of the Union were not ready to endorse Emancipation in 1861. In

1863, in the darkest hour of the war, the spirit of the North responded to the call, and, despite the vilification of the President, was true to him to victory. More significant still, in view of the events of today, is what then occurred in England. The British Government was unfriendly; the British people as a whole had looked upon our Civil War very much in the same light as the American people regarded the present war at its inception - which is to say that the economic and materialistic issue seemed to overshadow the moral one. When Abraham Lincoln proclaimed it to be a war for human freedom, the sentiment of the British people changed - of the British people as distinct from the governing classes; and the textile workers of the northern counties, whose mills could not get cotton on account of the blockade, declared their willingness to suffer and starve if the slaves in America might be freed.

Abraham Lincoln at that time represented the American people as the British Government did not represent the British people. We are concerned today with peoples rather than governments.

It remained for an American President to announce the moral issue of the present war, and thus to solidify behind him, not only the liberal mind of America, but the liberal elements within the nations of Europe. He became the democratic leader of the world. The issue, simply stated, is the advancement of democracy and peace. They are inseparable. Democracy, for progress, demands peace. It had reached a stage, when, in a contracting world, it could no longer advance through isolation: its very existence in every country was threatened, not only by the partisans of reaction from within, but by the menace from without of a militaristic and imperialistic nation determined to crush it, restore superimposed authority, and dominate the globe. Democracy, divided against itself, cannot stand. A league of democratic nations, of democratic peoples, has become imperative. Hereafter, if democracy wins, self-determination, and not imperialistic exploitation, is to be the universal rule. It is the extension, on a world scale, of Mr. Wilson's Mexican policy, the application of democratic principles to international relationships, and marks the inauguration of a new era. We resort to force against force, not for dominion, but to make the world safe for the idea on which we believe the future of civilization depends, the sacred right of self-government. We stand prepared to treat with the German people when they are ready to cast off autocracy and militarism. Our attitude toward them is precisely our attitude toward the Mexican People. We believe, and with good reason, that the German system of education is authoritative and false, and was more or less deliberately conceived in order to warp the nature and produce complexes in the mind of the German people for the end of preserving and perpetuating the power of the Junkers. We have no quarrel with the duped and oppressed, but we war against the agents of oppression. To the conservative mind such an aspiration appears chimerical. But America, youngest of the nations, was born when modern science was gathering the momentum which since has enabled it to overcome, with a bewildering rapidity, many evils previously held by superstition to be ineradicable. As a corollary to our democratic creed, we accepted the dictum that to human intelligence all things are possible. The virtue of this dictum lies not in dogma, but in an indomitable attitude of mind to which the world owes its every advance in civilization; quixotic, perhaps, but necessary to great accomplishment. In searching for a present-day protagonist, no happier example could be found than Mr. Henry Ford, who exhibits the characteristic American mixture of the practical and the ideal. He introduces into industry humanitarian practices that even tend to increase the vast fortune which by his own efforts he has accumulated. He sees that democratic peoples do not desire to go to war, he does not believe that war is necessary and inevitable, he lays himself open to ridicule by financing a Peace Mission. Circumstances force him to abandon his project, but he is not for one moment discouraged. His intention remains. He throws all his energy and wealth into a war to end war, and the value of his contribution is inestimable.

A study of Mr. Ford's mental processes and acts illustrates the true mind of America. In the autumn of 1916 Mr. Wilson declared that "the people of the United States want to be sure what they are fighting about, and they want to be sure that they are fighting for the things that will bring the world justice and peace. Define the elements; let us know that we are not fighting for the prevalence of this nation over that, for the ambitions of this group of nations as compared with the ambitions of that group of nations, let us once be convinced that we are called in to a great combination for the rights of mankind, and America will unite her force and spill her blood for the great things she has always believed in and followed."

"America is always ready to fight for the things which are American." Even in these sombre days that mark the anniversary of our entrance into the war. But let it be remembered that it was in the darkest days of the Civil War Abraham Lincoln boldly proclaimed the democratic, idealistic issue of that struggle. The Russian Revolution, which we must seek to understand and not condemn, the Allied defeats that are its consequences, can only make our purpose the firmer to put forth all our strength for the building up of a better world. The President's masterly series of state papers, distributed in all parts of the globe, have indeed been so many Proclamations of Emancipation for the world's oppressed. Not only powerful nations shall cease to exploit little nations, but powerful individuals shall cease to exploit their fellow men. Henceforth no wars for dominion shall be waged, and to this end secret treaties shall be abolished. Peoples through their representatives shall make their own treaties. And just as democracy insures to the individual the greatest amount of self-determination, nations also shall have self-determination, in order that each shall be free to make its world contribution. All citizens have duties to perform toward their fellow citizens; all democratic nations must be interdependent.

With this purpose America has entered the war. But it implies that our own household must be swept and cleaned. The injustices and inequalities existing in our own country, the false standards of worth, the materialism, the luxury and waste must be purged from our midst.

III

In fighting Germany we are indeed fighting an evil
Will - evil because it seeks to crush the growth of
individual and national freedom. Its object is to put the
world back under the thrall of self-constituted
authority. So long as this Will can compel the bodies
of soldiers to do its bidding, these bodies must be
destroyed. Until the Will behind them is broken, the
world cannot be free. Junkerism is the final expression
of reaction, organized to the highest efficiency. The
war against the Junkers marks the consummation of a
long struggle for human liberty in all lands, symbolizes
the real cleavage dividing the world. As in the French
Revolution and the wars that followed it, the true
significance of this war is social. But today the Russian
Revolution sounds the keynote. Revolutions tend to
express the extremes of the philosophies of their times
- human desires, discontents, and passions that cannot
be organized. The French Revolution was a struggle
for political freedom; the underlying issue of the
present war is economic freedom - without which
political freedom is of no account. It will not,
therefore, suffice merely to crush the Junkers, and with
them militarism and autocracy. Unless, as the fruit of
this appalling bloodshed and suffering, the
democracies achieve economic freedom, the war will
have been fought in vain. More revolutions, wastage
and bloodshed will follow, the world will be reduced

to absolute chaos unless, in the more advanced democracies, an intelligent social order tending to remove the causes of injustice and discontent can be devised and ready for inauguration. This new social order depends, in turn, upon a world order of mutually helpful, free peoples, a league of Nations. - If the world is to be made safe for democracy, this democratic plan must be ready for the day when the German Junker is beaten and peace is declared.

The real issue of our time is industrial democracy we must face that fact. And those in America and the Entente nations who continue to oppose it will do so at their peril. Fortunately, as will be shown, that element of our population which may be designated as domestic Junkers is capable of being influenced by contemporary currents of thought, is awakening to the realization of social conditions deplorable and dangerous. Prosperity and power had made them blind and arrogant. Their enthusiasm for the war was, however, genuine; the sacrifices they are making are changing and softening them; but as yet they can scarcely be expected, as a class, to rejoice over the revelation - just beginning to dawn upon their minds - that victory for the Allies spells the end of privilege. Their conception of democracy remains archaic, while wealth is inherently conservative. Those who possess it in America have as a rule received an education in terms of an obsolete economics, of the thought of an age gone by. It is only within the past few years that our colleges and universities have begun to teach modern economics, social science and psychology - and this in the face of opposition from trustees. Successful business men, as a rule, have had neither the time nor the inclination to read books which they regard as visionary, as subversive to an order by which they have profited. And that some Americans are fools, and have been dazzled in Europe by the glamour of a privilege not attainable at home, is a deplorable yet indubitable fact. These have little sympathy with democracy; they have even been heard to declare that we have no right to dictate to another nation, even an enemy nation, what form of government it shall assume. We have no right to demand, when peace comes, that the negotiations must be with the representatives of the German people. These are they who deplore the absence among us of a tradition of monarchy, since the American people "should have something to look up to." But this state of mind, which needs no comment, is comparatively rare, and represents an extreme. We are not lacking, however, in the type of conservative who, innocent of a knowledge of psychology, insists that "human nature cannot be changed," and that the "survival of the fittest" is the law of life, yet these would deny Darwin if he were a contemporary. They reject the idea that society can be organized by intelligence, and war ended by eliminating its causes from the social order. On the contrary they cling to the orthodox contention that war is a necessary and salutary thing, and proclaim that the American fibre was growing weak and flabby from luxury and peace, curiously ignoring the fact that their own economic class, the small percentage of our population owning sixty per cent. of the wealth of the country, and which therefore should be most debilitated by luxury, was most eager for war, and since war has been declared has most amply proved its courage and fighting quality. This, however, and other evidences of the patriotic sacrifices of those of our countrymen who possess wealth, prove that they are still Americans, and encourages the hope and belief that as Americans they ultimately will do their share toward a democratic solution of the problem of society. Many of them are capable of vision, and are beginning to see the light today.

In America we succeeded in eliminating hereditary power, in obtaining a large measure of political liberty, only to see the rise of an economic power, and the consequent loss of economic liberty. The industrial development of the United States was of course a necessary and desirable thing, but the economic doctrine which formed the basis of American institutions proved to be unsuited to industrialism, and introduced unforeseen evils that were a serious menace to the Republic. An individualistic economic philosophy worked admirably while there was ample land for the pioneer, equality of opportunity to satisfy the individual initiative of the enterprising. But what is known as industrialism brought in its train fear and favour, privilege and poverty, slums, disease, and municipal vice, fostered a too rapid immigration, established in America a tenant system alien to our traditions. The conditions which existed before the advent of industrialism are admirably pictured, for instance, in the autobiography of Mr. Charles Francis Adams, when he describes his native town of Quincy in the first half of the Nineteenth Century. In those early communities, poverty was negligible, there was no great contrast between rich and poor; the artisan, the farmer, the well-to-do merchant met on terms of mutual self-respect, as man to man; economic class consciousness was non-existent; education was so widespread that European travellers wonderingly commented on the fact that we had no "peasantry"; and with few exceptions every citizen owned a piece of land and a home. Property, a refuge a man may call his own, and on which he may express his individuality, is essential to happiness and self-respect. Today, less than two thirds of our farmers own their land, while vast numbers of our working men and women possess nothing but the labour of their hands. The designation of labour as "property" by our courts only served to tighten the bonds, by obstructing for a time the movement to decrease the tedious and debilitating hours of contact of the human organism with the machine, - a menace to the future of the race, especially in the case of women and children. If labour is "property," wretches driven by economic necessity have indeed only the choice of a change of masters. In addition to the manual workers, an army of clerical workers of both sexes likewise became tenants, and dependents who knew not the satisfaction of a real home.

Such conditions gradually brought about a profound discontent, a grouping of classes. Among the comparatively prosperous there was set up a social competition in luxury that was the bane of large and small communities. Skilled labour banded itself into unions, employers organized to oppose them, and the result was a class conflict never contemplated by the founders of the Republic, repugnant to democracy which by its very nature depends for its existence on the elimination of classes. In addition to this, owing to the unprecedented immigration of ignorant Europeans to supply the labour demand, we acquired a sinister proletariat of unskilled economic slaves. Before the war labour discovered its strength; since the war began, especially in the allied nations with quasi-democratic institutions, it is aware of its power to exert a leverage capable of paralyzing industry for a period sufficient to destroy the chances of victory. The probability of the occurrence of such a calamity depends wholly on whether or not the workman can be convinced that it is his war, for he will not exert himself to perpetuate a social order in which he has lost faith, even though he now obtains a considerable increase in wages. Agreements entered into with the government by union leaders will not hold him if at any time he fails to be satisfied that the present world conflict will not result in a greater social justice. This fact has been demonstrated by what is known as the "shop steward" movement in England, where the workers repudiated the leaders' agreements and everywhere organized local strikes. And in America, the unskilled workers are largely outside of the unions.

The workman has a natural and laudable desire to share more fully in the good things of life. And it is coming to be recognized that material prosperity, up to a certain point, is the foundation of mental and spiritual welfare: clean and comfortable surroundings, beauty, rational amusements, opportunity for a rational satisfaction of, the human. instincts are essential to contentment and progress. The individual, of course, must be enlightened; and local labour unions, recognizing this, are spending considerable sums all over the country on schools to educate their members. If a workman is a profiteer, he is more to be excused than the business profiteer, against whom his anger is directed; if he is a spendthrift, prodigality is a natural consequence of rapid acquisition. We have been a nation of spendthrifts.

A failure to grasp the psychology of the worker involves disastrous consequences. A discussion as to whether or not his attitude is unpatriotic and selfish is futile. No more profound mistake could be made than to attribute to any element of the population motives wholly base. Human nature is neither all black nor all white, yet is capable of supreme sacrifices when adequately appealed to. What we must get into our minds is the fact that a social order that insured a large measure of democracy in the early days of the Republic is inadequate to meet modern industrial conditions. Higher wages, material prosperity alone will not suffice to satisfy aspirations for a fuller self-realization, once the method by which these aspirations can be gained is glimpsed. For it cannot be too often repeated that the unquenchable conflicts are those waged for ideas and not dollars. These are tinged with religious emotion.

IV

Mr. Wilson's messages to the American people and to the world have proclaimed a new international order, a League of Democracies. And in a recent letter to New Jersey Democrats we find him warning his party, or more properly the nation, of the domestic social changes necessarily flowing from his international program. While rightly resolved to prosecute the war on the battle lines to the utmost limit of American resources, he points out that the true significance of the conflict lies in "revolutionary change." "Economic and social forces," he says, "are being released upon the world, whose effect no political seer dare to conjecture." And we "must search our hearts through and through and make them ready for the birth of a new day - a day we hope and believe of greater opportunity and greater prosperity for the average mass of struggling men and women." He recognizes that the next great step in the development of democracy which the war must bring about - is the emancipation of labour; to use his own phrase, the redemption of masses of men and women from "economic serfdom." "The old party slogans," he declares, "will mean nothing to the future."

Judging from this announcement, the President seems prepared to condemn boldly all the rotten timbers of the social structure that have outlived their usefulness -

a position that hitherto no responsible politician has dared to take. Politicians, on the contrary, have revered the dead wood, have sought to shore the old timbers for their own purposes. But so far as any party is concerned, Mr. Wilson stands alone. Both of the two great parties, the Republican and the Democratic, in order to make a show of keeping abreast of the times, have merely patched their platforms with the new ideas. The Socialist Party in the United States is relatively small, is divided against itself, and has given no evidence of a leadership of broad sanity and vision. It is fortunate we have been spared in this country the formation of a political labour party, because such a party would have been composed of manual workers alone, and hence would have tended further to develop economic class consciousness, to crystallize class antagonisms. Today, however, neither the Republican nor the Democratic party represents the great issue of the times; the cleavage between them is wholly artificial. The formation of a Liberal Party, with a platform avowedly based on modern social science, has become essential. Such a party, to be in harmony with our traditions and our creed, to arrest in our democracy the process of class stratification which threatens to destroy it, must not draw its members from the ranks of manual labour alone, but from all elements of our population. It should contain all the liberal professions, and clerks and shopkeepers, as well as manual workers; administrators, and even those employers who have become convinced that our present economic system does not suffice to meet the needs of the day. In short, membership in such a party, as far as possible, should not be based upon occupation or economic status, but on an honest difference of view from that of the conservative opposition. This would be a distinctly American solution. In order to form such a party a campaign of education will be necessary. For today Mr. Wilson's strength is derived from the independent vote representing the faith of the people as a whole; but the majority of those who support the President, while they ardently desire the abolition in the world of absolute monarchy, of militarism and commercial imperialism, while they are anxious that this war shall expedite and not retard the social reforms in which they are interested, have as yet but a vague conception of the social order which these reforms imply.

It marks a signal advance in democracy when liberal opinion in any nation turns for guidance and support to a statesman of another nation. No clearer sign of the times could be desired than the fact that our American President has suddenly become the liberal leader of the world. The traveller in France, and especially in Britain, meets on all sides striking evidence of this. In these countries, until America's entrance into the war, liberals had grown more and more dissatisfied with the failure of their governments to define in democratic terms the issue of the conflict, had resented the secret inter-allied compacts, savouring of imperialism and containing the germs of future war. They are now looking across the Atlantic for leadership. In France M. Albert Thomas declared that Woodrow Wilson had given voice to the aspirations of his party, while a prominent Liberal in England announced in a speech that it had remained for the American President to express the will and purpose of the British people. The new British Labour Party and the Inter-Allied Labour and Socialist Conferences have adopted Mr. Wilson's program and have made use of his striking phrases. But we have between America and Britain this difference: in America the President stands virtually alone, without a party behind him representing his views; in Britain the general democratic will of the nation is now being organized, but has obtained as yet no spokesman in the government.

Extraordinary symptomatic phenomena have occurred in Russia as well as in Britain. In Russia the rebellion of an awakening people against an age-long tyranny has almost at once leaped to the issue of the day, taken on the complexion of a struggle for industrial democracy. Whether the Germans shall be able to exploit the country, bring about a reaction and restore for a time monarchical institutions depends largely upon the fortunes of the war. In Russia there is revolution, with concomitant chaos; but in Britain there is evolution, an orderly attempt of a people long accustomed to progress in self-government to establish a new social order, peacefully and scientifically, and in accordance with a traditional political procedure.

The recent development of the British Labour Party, although of deep significance to Americans, has taken place almost without comment in this country. It was formally established in 1900, and was then composed of manual workers alone. In 1906, out of 50 candidates at the polls, 39 were elected to Parliament; in 1910, 42 were elected. The Parliamentary Labour Party, so called, has now been amalgamated with four and a half millions of Trade Unionists, and with the three and a half millions of members of the Co-operative Wholesale Society and the Co-operative Union. Allowing for duplication of membership, these three organizations - according to Mr. Sidney Webb - probably include two fifths of the population of the United Kingdom. "So great an aggregation of working class organizations," he says, "has never come shoulder to shoulder in any country." Other smaller societies and organizations are likewise embraced, including the Socialists. And now that the suffrage has been extended, provision is made for the inclusion of women. The new party is organizing in from three to four hundred constituencies, and at the next general election is not unlikely to gain control of the political balance of power.

With the majority of Americans, however, the word "labour" as designating a party arouses suspicion and distrust. By nature and tradition we are inclined to deplore and oppose any tendency toward the stratification of class antagonisms - the result of industrial discontent - into political groups. The British tradition is likewise hostile to such a tendency. But in Britain the industrial ferment has gone much further than with us, and such a result was inevitable. By taking advantage of the British experience, of the closer ties now being knit between the two democracies, we may in America be spared a stage which in Britain was necessary. Indeed, the program of the new British Labour Party seems to point to a distinctly American solution, one in harmony with the steady growth of Anglo-Saxon democracy. For it is now announced that the word "labour," as applied to the new party, does not mean manual labour alone, but also mental labour. The British unions have gradually developed and placed in power leaders educated in social science, who have now come into touch with the intellectual leaders of the United Kingdom, with the sociologists, economists, and social scientists. The surprising and encouraging result of such association is the announcement that the new Labour Party is today publicly thrown open to all workers, both by hand and by brain, with the object of securing for these the full fruits of their industry. This means the inclusion of physicians, professors, writers, architects, engineers, and inventors, of lawyers who no longer regard their profession as a bulwark of the status quo; of clerks, of administrators of the type evolved by the war, who indeed have gained their skill under the old order but who now in a social spirit are dedicating their gifts to the common weal, organizing and directing vast enterprises for their governments. In short, all useful citizens who make worthy contributions - as distinguished from parasites, profiteers, and drones, are invited to be members; there is no class distinction here. The fortunes of such a party are, of course, dependent upon the military success of the allied armies and navies. But it has defined the kind of democracy the Allies are fighting for, and thus has brought about an unqualified endorsement of the war by those elements of the population which hitherto have felt the issue to be imperialistic and vague rather than democratic and clear cut. President Wilson's international program is approved of and elaborated.

The Report on Reconstruction of the new British Labour Party is perhaps the most important political document presented to the world since the Declaration of Independence. And like the Declaration, it is written in the pure English that alone gives the high emotional quality of sincerity. The phrases in which it tersely describes its objects are admirable. "What is to be reconstructed after the war is over is not this or that government department, this or that piece of social machinery, but Society itself." There is to be a systematic approach towards a "healthy equality of material circumstance for every person born into the world, and not an enforced dominion over subject nations, subject colonies, subject classes, or a subject sex." In industry as well as in government the social order is to be based "on that equal freedom, that general consciousness of consent, and that widest participation in power, both economic and political, which is characteristic of democracy." But all this, it should be noted, is not to be achieved in a year or two of "feverish reconstruction"; "each brick that the Labour Party helps to lay shall go to erect the structure it intends and no other."

In considering the main features of this program, one must have in mind whether these are a logical projection and continuation of the Anglo-Saxon democratic tradition, or whether they constitute an absolute break with that tradition. The only valid reason for the adoption of such a program in America would be, of course, the restoration of some such equality of opportunity and economic freedom as existed in our Republic before we became an industrial nation. "The first condition of democracy," - to quote again from the program, "is effective personal freedom."

What is called the "Universal Enforcement of the National Minimum" contemplates the extension of laws already on the statute books in order to prevent the extreme degradation of the standard of life brought about by the old economic system under industrialism. A living minimum wage is to be established. The British Labour Party intends "to secure to every member of the community, in good times and bad alike . . . all the requisites of healthy life and worthy citizenship."

After the war there is to be no cheap labour market, nor are the millions of workers and soldiers to fall into the clutches of charity; but it shall be a national obligation to provide each of these with work according to his capacity. In order to maintain the demand for labour at a uniform level, the government is to provide public works. The population is to be rehoused in suitable dwellings, both in rural districts and town slums; new and more adequate schools and training colleges are to be inaugurated; land is to be reclaimed and afforested, and gradually brought under common ownership; railways and canals are to be reorganized and nationalized, mines and electric power systems. One of the significant proposals under this head is that which demands the retention of the centralization of the purchase of raw materials brought about by the war.

In order to accomplish these objects there must be a "Revolution in National Finance." The present method of raising funds is denounced; and it is pointed out that only one quarter of the colossal expenditure made necessary by the war has been raised by taxation, and that the three quarters borrowed at onerous rates is sure to be a burden on the nation's future. The capital needed, when peace comes, to ensure a happy and contented democracy must be procured without encroaching on the minimum standard of life, and without hampering production. Indirect taxation must therefore be concentrated on those luxuries of which it is desirable that the consumption be discouraged. The steadily rising unearned increment of urban and mineral land ought, by appropriate direct taxation, to be brought into the public exchequer; "the definite teachings of economic science are no longer to be disregarded." Hence incomes are to be taxed above the necessary cost of family maintenance, private fortunes during life and at death; while a special capital levy must be made to pay off a substantial portion of the national debt.

"The Democratic Control of Industry" contemplates the progressive elimination of the private capitalist and the setting free of all who work by hand and brain for the welfare of all.

The Surplus Wealth is to be expended for the Common Good. That which Carlyle designates as the "inward spiritual," in contrast to the "outward economical," is also to be provided for. "Society," says the document, "like the individual, does not live by bread alone, does not exist only for perpetual wealth production." First of all, there is to be education according to the highest modern standard; and along with education, the protection and advancement of the public health, 'mens sana in corpore sano'. While large sums must be set aside, not only for original research in every branch of knowledge, but for the promotion of music, literature, and fine art, upon which "any real development of civilization fundamentally depends."

In regard to the British Empire, the Labour Party urges self-government for any people, whatever its colour, proving itself capable, and the right of that people to the proceeds of its own toil upon the resources of its territory. An unequivocal stand is taken for the establishment, as a part of the treaty of peace, of a Universal Society of Nations; and recognizing that the future progress of democracy depends upon co-operation and fellowship between liberals of all countries, the maintenance of intimate relationships is advocated with liberals oversea.

Finally, a scientific investigation of each succeeding

problem in government is insisted upon, and a much more rapid dissemination among the people of the science that exists. "A plutocratic party may choose to ignore science, but no labour party can hope to maintain its position unless its proposals are, in fact, the outcome of the best political science of its time."

V

There are, it will be seen, some elements in the program of the new British Labour Party apparently at variance with American and English institutions, traditions, and ideas. We are left in doubt, for instance, in regard to its attitude toward private property. The instinct for property is probably innate in humanity, and American conservatism in this regard is, according to certain modern economists, undoubtedly sound. A man should be permitted to acquire at least as much property as is required for the expression of his personality; such a wise limitation, also, would abolish the evil known as absentee ownership. Again, there will arise in many minds the question whether the funds for the plan of National finance outlined in the program may be obtained without seriously deranging the economic system of the nation and of the world. The older school denounces the program as Utopian. On the other hand, economists of the modern school who have been consulted have declared it practical. It is certain that before the war began it would not have been thought possible to raise the billions which in four years have been expended on sheer destruction; and one of our saddest reflections today must be of regret that a small portion of these billions which have gone to waste could not have been expended for the very purposes outlined - education, public health, the advancement of science and art, public buildings, roads and parks, and the proper housing of populations! It is also dawning upon us, as a result of new practices brought about by the war, that our organization of industry was happy-go-lucky, inefficient and wasteful, and that a more scientific and economical organization is imperative. Under such a new system it may well be, as modern economists claim, that, we shall have an ample surplus for the Common Good.

The chief objection to a National or Democratic Control of Industry has been that it would tend to create vast political machines and thus give the politicians in office a nefarious power. It is not intended here to attempt a refutation of this contention. The remedy lies in a changed attitude of the employee and the citizen toward government, and the fact that such an attitude is now developing is not subject to absolute proof. It may be said, however, that no greater menace to democracy could have arisen than the one we seem barely to have escaped - the control of politics and government by the capitalistic interests of the nation. What seems very clear is that an evolutionary drift toward the national control of industry has for many years been going on, and that the war has tremendously speeded up the tendency. Government has stepped in to protect the consumer of necessities from the profiteer, and is beginning to set a limit upon profits; has regulated exports and imports; established a national shipping corporation and merchant marine, and entered into other industries; it has taken over the railroads at least for the duration of the war, and may take over coal mines, and metal resources, as well as the forests and water power; it now contemplates the regulation of wages.

The exigency caused by the war, moreover, has

transformed the former practice of international intercourse. Co-operation has replaced competition. We are reorganizing and regulating our industries, our business, making sacrifices and preparing to make more sacrifices in order to meet the needs of our Allies, now that they are sore beset. For a considerable period after the war is ended, they will require our aid. We shall be better off than any other of the belligerent nations, and we shall therefore be called upon to practice, during the years of reconstruction, a continuation of the same policy of helpfulness. Indeed, for the nations of the world to spring, commercially speaking, at one another's throats would be suicidal even if it were possible. Mr. Sidney Webb has thrown a flood of light upon the conditions likely to prevail. For example, speculative export trade is being replaced by collective importing, bringing business more directly under the control of the consumer. This has been done by co-operative societies, by municipalities and states, in Switzerland, France, the United Kingdom, and in Germany. The Co-operative Wholesale Society of Great Britain, acting on behalf of three and a half million families, buys two and a half million dollars of purchases annually. And the Entente nations, in order to avoid competitive bidding, are buying collectively from us, not only munitions of war, but other supplies, while the British Government has made itself the sole importer of such necessities as wheat, sugar, tea, refrigerated meat, wool, and various metals. The French and Italian governments, and also certain neutral states, have done likewise. A purchasing commission for all the Allies and America is now proposed. After the war, as an inevitable result, for one thing, of transforming some thirty million citizens into soldiers, of engaging a like number of men and women at enhanced wages on the manufacture of the requisites of war, Mr. Webb predicts a world shortage not only in wheat and foodstuffs but in nearly all important raw materials. These will be required for the resumption of manufacture. In brief, international co-operation will be the only means of salvation. The policy of international trade implied by world shortage is not founded upon a law of "supply and demand." The necessities cannot be permitted to go to those who can afford to pay the highest prices, but to those who need them most. For the "free play of economic forces" would mean famine on a large scale, because the richer nations and the richer classes within the nations might be fully supplied; but to the detriment and ruin of the world the poorer nations and the poorer classes would be starved. Therefore governments are already beginning to give consideration to a new organization of international trade for at least three years after the war. Now if this organization produce, as it may produce, a more desirable civilization and a happier world order, we are not likely entirely to go back - especially in regard to commodities which are necessities - to a competitive system. The principle of "priority of need" will supersede the law of "supply and demand." And the organizations built up during the war, if they prove efficient, will not be abolished. Hours of labour and wages in the co-operative League of Nations will gradually be equalized, and tariffs will become things of the past. "The axiom will be established," says Mr. Webb, "that the resources of every country must, be held for the benefit not only of its own people but of the world . . . . The world shortage will, for years to come, make import duties look both oppressive and ridiculous."

So much may be said for the principle of Democratic

Control. In spite of all theoretical opposition, circumstances and evolution apparently point to its establishment. A system that puts a premium on commercial greed seems no longer possible.

The above comments, based on the drift of political practice during the past decade and a half, may be taken for what they are worth. Predictions are precarious. The average American will be inclined to regard the program of the new British Labour Party as the embodiment of what he vaguely calls Socialism, and to him the very word is repugnant. Although he may never have heard of Marx, it is the Marxian conception that comes to his mind, and this implies coercion, a government that constantly interferes with his personal liberty, that compels him to tasks for which he has no relish. But your American, and your Englishman, for that matter, is inherently an individualist he wants as little government as is compatible with any government at all. And the descendants of the continental Europeans who flock to our shores are Anglo-Saxonized, also become by environment and education individualists. The great importance of preserving this individualism, this spirit in our citizens of selfreliance, this suspicion against too much interference with personal liberty, must at once be admitted. And any scheme for a social order that tends to eliminate and destroy it should by Americans be summarily rejected.

The question of supreme interest to us, therefore, is whether the social order implied in the British program is mainly in the nature of a development of, or a break with, the Anglo-Saxon democratic tradition. The program is derived from an English source. It is based on what is known as modern social science, which has as its ultimate sanction the nature of the human mind as revealed by psychology. A consideration of the principles underlying this proposed social order may prove that it is essentially - if perhaps paradoxically - individualistic, a logical evolution of institutions which had their origin in the Magna Charta. Our Declaration of Independence proclaimed that every citizen had the right to "life, liberty, and the pursuit of happiness," which means the opportunity to achieve the greatest self-development and self-realization. The theory is that each citizen shall find his place, according to his gifts and abilities, and be satisfied therewith. We may discover that this is precisely what social science, in an industrial age, and by spiritualizing human effort, aims to achieve. We may find that the appearance of such a program as that of the British Labour Party, supported as it is by an imposing proportion of the population of the United Kingdom, marks a further step, not only in the advance of social science and democracy, but also of Christianity.

I mention Christianity, not for controversial or apologetic reasons, but because it has been the leaven of our western civilization ever since the fall of the Roman Empire. Its constant influence has been to soften and spiritualize individual and national relationships. The bitter controversies, wars, and persecutions which have raged in its name are utterly alien to its being. And that the present war is now being fought by the Allies in the hope of putting an end to war, and is thus in the true spirit of Christianity, marks an incomparable advance.

Almost up to the present day, both in our conception and practice of Christianity, we have largely neglected its most important elements. Christian orthodoxy, as

Auguste Sabatier points out, is largely derived from the older supernatural religions. The preservative shell of dogma and superstition has been cracking, and is now ready to burst, and the social teaching of Jesus would seem to be the kernel from which has sprung modern democracy, modern science, and modern religion - a trinity and unity.

For nearly two thousand years orthodoxy has insisted that the social principles of Christianity are impractical. And indeed, until the present day, they have been so. Physical science, by enormously accelerating the means of transportation and communication, has so contracted the world as to bring into communion peoples and races hitherto far apart; has made possible an intelligent organization of industry which, for the first time in history, can create a surplus ample to maintain in comfort the world's population. But this demands the will to co-operation, which is a Christian principle - a recognition of the brotherhood of man. Furthermore, physical science has increased the need for world peace and international co-operation because the territories of all nations are now subject to swift and terrible invasion by modern instruments of destruction, while the future submarine may sweep commerce from the seas.

Again, orthodoxy declares that human nature is inherently "bad," while true Christianity, endorsed by psychology, proclaims it inherently "good," which means that, properly guided, properly educated, it is creative and contributive rather than destructive. No more striking proof of this fact can be cited than the modern experiment in prison reform in which hardened convicts, when "given a chance," frequently become useful citizens. Unjust and unintelligent social conditions are the chief factors in making criminals.

Our most modern system of education, of which Professor John Dewey is the chief protagonist, is based upon the assertions of psychology that human nature is essentially "good" creative. Every normal child is supposed to have a special "distinction" or gift, which it is the task of the educator to discover. This distinction found, the child achieves happiness in creation and contribution. Self-realization demands knowledge and training: the doing of right is not a negative but a positive act; it is not without significance that the Greek word for sin is literally "missing the mark." Christianity emphasizes above all else the worth of the individual, yet recognizes that the individual can develop only in society. And if the individual be of great worth, this worth must be by society developed to its utmost. Universal suffrage is a logical corollary.

Universal suffrage, however, implies individual judgment, which means that the orthodox principle of external authority is out of place both in Christianity and democracy. The Christian theory is that none shall intervene between a man's Maker and himself; democracy presupposes that no citizen shall accept his beliefs and convictions from others, but shall make up his own mind and act accordingly. Open-mindedness is the first requisite of science and democracy.

What has been deemed, however, in Christianity the most unrealizable ideal is that which may be called pacifism - to resist not evil, to turn the other cheek, to agree with your adversary while you are in the way with him. "I come not," said Jesus, in one of those paradoxical statements hitherto so difficult to understand, "I come not to bring peace, but a sword." It is indeed what we are fighting for - peace. But we believe today, more strongly than ever before, as democracy advances, as peoples tend to gain more and more control over their governments, that even this may not be an unrealizable ideal. Democracies, intent on self-realization and self-development, do not desire war.

The problem of social science, then, appears to be to organize human society on the principles and ideals of Christianity. But in view of the fact that the trend of evolution is towards the elimination of commercial competition, the question which must seriously concern us today is - What in the future shall be the spur of individual initiative? Orthodoxy and even democratic practice have hitherto taken it for granted - in spite of the examples of highly socialized men, benefactors of society - that the average citizen will bestir himself only for material gain. And it must be admitted that competition of some sort is necessary for self-realization, that human nature demands a prize. There can be no self-sacrifice without a corresponding self-satisfaction. The answer is that in the theory of democracy, as well as in that of Christianity, individualism and co-operation are paradoxically blended. For competition, Christianity substitutes emulation. And with democracy, it declares that mankind itself can gradually be rained towards the level of the choice individual who does not labour for gain, but in behalf of society. For the process of democracy is not degrading, but lifting. Like Christianity, democracy demands faith, and has as its inspiring interpretation of civilization evolution towards a spiritual goal. Yet the kind of faith required is no longer a blind faith, but one founded on sane and carefully evolved theories. Democracy has become a scientific experiment.

In this connection, as one notably inspired by emulation, by the joy of creative work and service, the medical profession comes first to mind. The finer element in this profession is constantly increasing in numbers, growing more and more influential, making life less easy for the quack, the vendor of nostrums, the commercial proprietor of the bogus medical college. The doctor who uses his talents for gain is frowned upon by those of his fellow practitioners whose opinion really counts. Respected physicians in our cities give much of their time to teaching, animating students with their own spirit; and labour long hours, for no material return, in the clinics of the poor. And how often, in reading our newspapers, do we learn that some medical scientist, by patient work, and often at the risk of life and health, has triumphed over a scourge which has played havoc with humanity throughout the ages! Typhoid has been conquered, and infant paralysis; gangrene and tetanus, which have taken such toll of the wounded in Flanders and France; yellow fever has been stamped out in the tropics; hideous lesions are now healed by a system of drainage. The very list of these achievements is bewildering, and latterly we are given hope of the prolongation of life itself. Here in truth are Christian deeds multiplied by science, made possible by a growing knowledge of and mastery over Nature.

Such men by virtue of their high mission are above the vicious social and commercial competition poisoning the lives of so many of their fellow citizens. In our democracy they have found their work, and the work is its own reward. They give striking testimony to the theory that absorption in a creative or contributive task is the only source of self-realization. And he has little faith in mankind who shall declare that the medical profession is the only group capable of being socialized, or, rather, of socializing themselves - for such is the true process of democracy. Public opinion should be the leaven. What is possible for the doctor is also possible for the lawyer, for the teacher. In a democracy, teaching should be the most honoured of the professions, and indeed once was, - before the advent of industrialism, when it gradually fell into neglect, - occasionally into deplorable submission to the possessors of wealth. Yet a wage disgracefully low, hardship, and even poverty have not hindered men of ability from entering it in increasing numbers, renouncing ease and luxuries. The worth of the contributions of our professors to civilization has been inestimable; and fortunately signs are not lacking that we are coming to an appreciation of the value of the expert in government, who is replacing the panderer and the politician. A new solidarity of teaching professional opinion, together with a growing realization by our public of the primary importance of the calling, is tending to emancipate it, to establish it in its rightful place.

Nor are our engineers without their ideal. A Goethals did not cut an isthmus in two for gain.

Industrialism, with its concomitant "corporation" practice, has undoubtedly been detrimental to the legal profession, since it has resulted in large fees; in the accumulation of vast fortunes, frequently by methods ethically questionable. Grave social injustices have been done, though often in good faith, since the lawyer, by training and experience, has hitherto been least open to the teachings of the new social science, has been an honest advocate of the system of 'laissez faire'. But to say that the American legal profession is without ideals and lacking in the emulative spirit would be to do it a grave injustice. The increasing influence of national and state bar associations evidences a professional opinion discouraging to the unscrupulous; while a new evolutionary and more humanitarian conception of law is now beginning to be taught, and young men are entering the ranks imbued with this. Legal clinics, like medical clinics, are established for the benefit of those who cannot afford to pay fees, for the protection of the duped from the predatory quack. And, it must be said of this profession, which hitherto has held a foremost place in America, that its leaders have never hesitated to respond to a public call, to sacrifice their practices to serve the nation. Their highest ambition has even been to attain the Supreme Court, where the salary is a mere pittance compared to what they may earn as private citizens.

Thus we may review all the groups in the nation, but the most significant transformation of all is taking place within the business group, - where indeed it might be least expected. Even before the war there were many evidences that the emulative spirit in business had begun to modify the merely competitive, and eve had the spectacle of large employers of labour awakening to the evils of industrialism, and themselves attempting to inaugurate reforms. As in the case of labour, it would be obviously unfair to claim that the employer element was actuated by motives of self-interest alone; nor were their concessions due only to fear. Instances could be cited, if there were space, of voluntary shortening of hours of labour, of raising of wages, when no coercion was exerted either by the labour unions or the state; and - perhaps to their surprise employers discovered that such acts were not only humane but profitable! Among these employers, in fact, may be observed individuals in various stages of enlightenment, from the few who have educated themselves in social science, who are convinced that the time has come when it is not only practicable but right, who realize that a new era has dawned; to others who still believe in the old system, who are trying to bolster it up by granting concessions, by establishing committees of conference, by giving a voice and often a financial interest, but not a vote, in the conduct of the corporation concerned. These are the counterpart, in industry, of sovereigns whose away has been absolute, whose intentions are good, but who hesitate, often from conviction, to grant constitutions. Yet even these are responding in some degree to social currents, though the aggressive struggles of labour may have influenced them, and partially opened their eyes. They are far better than their associates who still seek to control the supplies of food and other necessities, whose efficiency is still solely directed, not toward a social end, but toward the amassing of large fortunes, and is therefore wasted so far as society is concerned. They do not perceive that by seeking to control prices they merely hasten the tendency of government control, for it is better to have government regulation for the benefit of the many than proprietary control, however efficient, for the benefit of the few.

That a significant change of heart and mind has begun to take place amongst capitalists, that the nucleus of a "public opinion" has been formed within an element which, by the use and wont of business and habits of thought might be regarded as least subject to the influence of social ideas, is a most hopeful augury. This nascent opinion has begun to operate by shaming unscrupulous and recalcitrant employers into better practices. It would indeed fare ill with democracy if, in such an era, men of large business proved to be lacking in democratic initiative, wholly unreceptive and hostile to the gradual introduction of democracy into industry, which means the perpetuation of the American Idea. Fortunately, with us, this capitalistic element is of comparatively recent growth, the majority of its members are essentially Americans; they have risen from small beginnings, and are responsive to a democratic appeal - if that appeal be properly presented. And, as a matter of fact, for many years a leaven had been at work among them; the truth has been brought home to them that the mere acquisition of wealth brings neither happiness nor self-realization; they have lavished their money on hospitals and universities, clinics, foundations for scientific research, and other gifts of inestimable benefit to the nation and mankind. Although the munificence was on a Medicean scale, this private charity was in accord with the older conception of democracy, and paved the way for a new order.

The patriotic and humanitarian motive aroused by the war greatly accelerated the socializing transformation of the business man and the capitalist. We have, indeed, our profiteers seeking short cuts to luxury and wealth; but those happily most representative of American affairs, including the creative administrators, hastened to Washington with a willingness to accept any position in which they might be useful, and in numerous instances placed at the disposal of the government the manufacturing establishments which, by industry and ability, they themselves had built up.

That in thus surrendering the properties for which they were largely responsible they hoped at the conclusion of peace to see restored the 'status quo ante' should not be held against them. Some are now beginning to surmise that a complete restoration is impossible; and as a result of their socializing experience, are even wondering whether it is desirable. These are beginning to perceive that the national and international organizations in the course of construction to meet the demands of the world conflict must form the model for a future social structure; that the unprecedented pressure caused by the cataclysm is compelling a recrystallization of society in which there must be fewer misfits, in which many more individuals than formerly shall find public or semi-public tasks in accordance with their gifts and abilities.

It may be argued that war compels socialization, that after the war the world will perforce return to materia-listic individualism. But this calamity, terrible above all others, has warned us of the imperative need of an order that shall be socializing, if we are not to witness the destruction of our civilization itself. Confidence that such an order, thanks to the advancement of science, is now within our grasp should not be difficult for Americans, once they have rightly conceived it. We, who have always pinned our faith to ideas, who entered the conflict for an Idea, must be the last to shirk the task, however Herculean, of world reconstruction along the lines of our own professed faith. We cannot be renegades to Democracy.

Above all things, then, it is essential for us as a people not to abandon our faith in man, our belief that not only the exceptional individual but the majority of mankind can be socialized. What is true of our physicians, our scientists and professional men, our manual workers, is also true of our capitalists and business men. In a more just and intelligent organization of society these will be found willing to administer and improve for the common weal the national resources which formerly they exploited for the benefit of themselves and their associates. The social response, granted the conditions, is innate in humanity, and individual initiative can best be satisfied in social realization.

Universal education is the cornerstone of democracy. And the recognition of this fact may be called the great American contribution. But in our society the fullest self-realization depends upon a well balanced knowledge of scientific facts, upon a rounded culture. Thus education, properly conceived, is a preparation for intelligent, ethical, and contented citizenship. Upon the welfare of the individual depends the welfare of all. Without education, free institutions and universal suffrage are mockeries; semi-learned masses of the population are at the mercy of scheming politicians, controversialists, and pseudo-scientific religionists, and their votes are swayed by prejudice.

In a materialistic competitive order, success in life depends upon the knack - innate or acquired, and not to be highly rated - of outwitting one's neighbour under the rules of the game - the law; education is merely a cultural leaven within the reach of the comparatively few who can afford to attend a university. The business college is a more logical institution. In an emulative civilization, however, the problem is to discover and develop in childhood and youth the personal aptitude or gift of as many citizens as possible, in order that they may find self-realization by making their peculiar contribution towards the advancement of society.

The prevailing system of education, which we have inherited from the past, largely fails to accomplish this. In the first place, it has been authoritative rather than scientific, which is to say that students have been induced to accept the statements of teachers and text books, and have not been trained to weigh for themselves their reasonableness and worth; a principle essentially unscientific and undemocratic, since it inculcates in the future citizen convictions rather than encourages the habit of openmindedness so necessary for democratic citizenship. For democracy - it cannot be too often repeated - is a dynamic thing, experimental, creative in its very essence. No static set of opinions can apply to the constantly changing aspect of affairs. New discoveries, which come upon us with such bewildering rapidity, are apt abruptly to alter social and industrial conditions, while morals and conventions are no longer absolute. Sudden crises threaten the stability of nations and civilizations. Safety lies alone in the ability to go forward, to progress. Psychology teaches us that if authoritative opinions, convictions, or "complexes" are stamped upon the plastic brain of the youth they tend to harden, and he is apt to become a Democrat or Republican, an Episcopalian or a Baptist, a free trader or a tariff advocate or a Manchester economist without asking why. Such "complexes" were probably referred to by the celebrated physician who emphasized the hopelessness of most individuals over forty. And every reformer and forum lecturer knows how difficult it is to convert the average audience of seasoned adults to a new idea: he finds the most responsive groups in the universities and colleges. It is significant that the "educated" adult audiences in clubs and prosperous churches are the least open to conversion, because, in the scientific sense, the "educated" classes retain complexes, and hence are the least prepared to cope with the world as it is today. The German system, which has been bent upon installing authoritative conviction instead of encouraging freedom of thought, should be a warning to us.

Again, outside of the realm of physical science, our text books have been controversial rather than impartial, especially in economics and history; resulting in erroneous and distorted and prejudiced ideas of events, such for instance, as our American Revolution. The day of the controversialist is happily coming to an end, and of the writer who twists the facts of science to suit a world of his own making, or of that of a group with which he is associated. Theory can now be labelled theory, and fact, fact. Impartial and painstaking investigation is the sole method of obtaining truth.

The old system of education benefited only the comparatively few to whose nature and inclination it was adapted. We have need, indeed, of classical scholars, but the majority of men and women are meant for other work; many, by their very construction of mind, are unfitted to become such. And only in the most exceptional cases are the ancient languages really mastered; a smattering of these, imposed upon the unwilling scholar by a principle opposed to psychology, - a smattering from which is derived no use and joy in after life, and which has no connection with individual inclination - is worse than nothing. Precious time is wasted during the years when the mind is most receptive. While the argument of the old school that discipline can only be inculcated by the imposition of a distasteful task is unsound. As Professor Dewey points out, unless the interest is in some way involved there can be no useful discipline. And how many of our university and high school graduates today are in any sense disciplined? Stimulated interest alone can overcome the resistance imposed by a difficult task, as any scientist, artist, organizer or administrator knows. Men will discipline themselves to gain a desired end. Under the old system of education a few children succeed either because they are desirous of doing well, interested in the game of mental competition; or else because they contrive to clothe with flesh and blood some subject presented as a skeleton. It is not uncommon, indeed, to recognize in later years with astonishment a useful citizen or genius whom at school or college we recall as a dunce or laggard. In our present society, because of archaic methods of education, the development of such is largely left to chance. Those who might have been developed in time, who might have found their task, often become wasters, drudges, and even criminals.

The old system tends to make types, to stamp every scholar in the same mould, whether he fits it or not. More and more the parents of today are looking about for new schools, insisting that a son or daughter possesses some special gift which, under teachers of genius, might be developed before it is too late. And in most cases, strange to say, the parents are right. They themselves have been victims of a standardized system.

A new and distinctly American system of education, designed to meet the demands of modern conditions, has been put in practice in parts of the United States. In spite of opposition from school boards, from all those who cling to the conviction that education must of necessity be an unpalatable and "disciplinary" process, the number of these schools is growing. The objection, put forth by many, that they are still in the experimental stage, is met by the reply that experiment is the very essence of the system. Democracy is experimental, and henceforth education will remain experimental for all time. But, as in any other branch of science, the element of ascertained fact will gradually increase: the latent possibilities in the mind of the healthy child will be discovered by knowledge gained through impartial investigation. The old system, like all other institutions handed down to us from the ages, proceeds on no intelligent theory, has no basis on psychology, and is accepted merely because it exists.

The new education is selective. The mind of each child is patiently studied with the view of discovering the peculiar bent, and this bent is guided and encouraged. The child is allowed to forge ahead in those subjects for which he shows an aptitude, and not compelled to wait on a class. Such supervision, of course, demands more teachers, teachers of an ability hitherto deplorably rare, and thoroughly trained in their subjects, with a sympathetic knowledge of the human mind. Theirs will be the highest and most responsible function in the state, and they must be rewarded in proportion to their services.

A superficial criticism declares that in the new schools children will study only "what they like." On the contrary, all subjects requisite for a wide culture, as well as for the ability to cope with existence in a highly complex civilization, are insisted upon. It is true, however, that the trained and gifted teacher is able to discover a method of so presenting a subject as to seize the imagination and arouse the interest and industry of a majority of pupils. In the modern schools French, for example, is really taught; pupils do not acquire a mere smattering of the language. And, what is more important, the course of study is directly related to life, and to practical experience, instead of being set forth abstractly, as something which at the time the pupil perceives no possibility of putting into use. At one of the new schools in the south, the ignorant child of the mountains at once acquires a knowledge of measurement and elementary arithmetic by laying out a garden, of letters by inscribing his name on a little signboard in order to identify his patch - for the moment private property. And this principle is carried through all the grades. In the Gary Schools and elsewhere the making of things in the shops, the modelling of a Panama Canal, the inspection of industries and governmental establishments, the designing, building, and decoration of houses, the discussion and even dramatization of the books read, - all are a logical and inevitable continuation of the abstract knowledge of the schoolroom. The success of the direct application of learning to industrial and professional life may also be observed in such colleges as those at Cincinnati and Schenectady, where young men spend half the time of the course in the shops of manufacturing, corporations, often earning more than enough to pay their tuition.

Children are not only prepared for democratic citizenship by being encouraged to think for themselves, but also to govern and discipline themselves. On the moral side, under the authoritative system of lay and religious training, character was acquired at the expense of mental flexibility - the Puritan method; our problem today, which the new system undertakes, is to produce character with openmindedness - the kind of character possessed by many great scientists. Absorption in an appropriate task creates a moral will, while science, knowledge, informs the mind why a thing is "bad" or "good," disintegrating or upbuilding. Moreover, these children are trained for democratic government by the granting of autonomy. They have their own elected officials, their own courts; their decisions are, of course, subject to reversal by the principal, but in practice this seldom occurs.

The Gary Schools and many of the new schools are public schools. And the principle of the new education that the state is primarily responsible for the health of pupils - because an unsound body is apt to make an unsound citizen of backward intelligence - is now being generally adopted by public schools all over the country. This idea is essentially an element of the democratic contention that all citizens must be given an equality of opportunity - though all may not be created equal - now becoming a positive rather than a negative right, guaranteed by the state itself. An earnest attempt is thus made by the state to give every citizen a fair start that in later years he may have no ground for discontent or complaint. He stands on his own feet, he rises in proportion to his ability and industry. Hence the program of the British Labour Party rightly lays stress on education, on "freedom of mental opportunity." The vast sums it proposes to spend for this purpose are justified.

If such a system of education as that briefly outlined above is carefully and impartially considered, the objection that democratic government founded on modern social science is coercive must disappear. So far as the intention and effort of the state is able to confer it, every citizen will have his choice of the task he is to perform for society, his opportunity for self-realization. For freedom without education is a myth. By degrees men and women are making ready to take their places in an emulative rather than a materialistically competitive order. But the experimental aspect of this system should always be borne in mind, with the fact that its introduction and progress, like that of other elements in the democratic program, must be gradual, though always proceeding along sound lines. For we have arrived at that stage of enlightenment when we realize that the only mundane perfection lies in progress rather than achievement. The millennium is always a lap ahead. There would be no satisfaction in overtaking it, for then we should have nothing more to do, nothing more to work for.

The German Junkers have prostituted science by employing it for the destruction of humanity. In the name of Christianity they have waged the most barbaric war in history. Yet if they shall have demonstrated to mankind the futility of efficiency achieved merely for material ends; if, by throwing them on a world screen, they shall have revealed the evils of power upheld alone by ruthlessness and force, they will unwittingly have performed a world service. Privilege and dominion, powers and principalities acquired by force must be sustained by force. To fail will be fatal. Even a duped people, trained in servility, will not consent to be governed by an unsuccessful autocracy. Arrogantly Germany has staked her all on world domination. Hence a victory for the Allies must mean a democratic Germany.

Nothing short of victory. There can be no arrangement, no agreement, no parley with or confidence in these modern scions of darkness - Hohenzollerns, Hindenburgs, Zudendorffs and their tools. Propaganda must not cease; the eyes of Germans still capable of sight must be opened. But, as the President says, force must be used to the limit - force for a social end as opposed to force for an evil end. There are those among us who advocate a boycott of Germany after peace is declared. These would seem to take it for granted that we shall fall short of victory, and hence that selfish retaliative or vindictive practices between nations, sanctioned by imperialism, will continue to flourish after the war. But should Germany win she will see to it that there is no boycott against her. A compromised peace would indeed mean the perpetuation of both imperialism and militarism.

It is characteristic of those who put their faith in might alone that they are not only blind to the finer relationships between individuals and nations, but take no account of the moral forces in human affairs which in the long run are decisive, - a lack of sensitiveness which explains Germany's colossal blunders. The first had to do with Britain. The German militarists persisted in the belief that the United Kingdom was degenerated by democracy, intent upon the acquisition of wealth, distracted by strife at home, uncertain of the Empire, and thus would selfishly remain aloof while the Kaiser's armies overran and enslaved the continent. What happened, to Germany's detriment, was the instant socialization of Britain, and the binding together of the British Empire. Germany's second great blunder was an arrogant underestimation of a self-reliant people of English culture and traditions. She believed that we, too, had been made flabby by democracy, were wholly intent upon the pursuit of the dollar - only to learn that America would lavish her vast resources and shed her blood for a cause which was American. Germany herself provided that cause, shaped the issues so that there was no avoiding them. She provided the occasion for the socializing of America also; and thus brought about, within a year, a national transformation which in times of peace might scarce in half a century have been accomplished.

Above all, as a consequence of these two blunders, Germany has been compelled to witness the consummation of that which of all things she had most to fear, the cementing of a lasting fellowship between the English speaking Republic and the English speaking Empire. For we had been severed since the 18th Century by misunderstandings which of late Germany herself had been more or less successful in fostering. She has furnished a bond not only between our governments, but - what is vastly more important for democracy - a bond between our peoples. Our soldiers are now side by side with those of the Empire on the Frontier of Freedom; the blood of all is shed and mingled for a great cause embodied in the Anglo-Saxon tradition of democracy; and our peoples, through the realization of common ideas and common ends, are learning the supreme lesson of co-operation between nations with a common past, are being cemented into a union which is the symbol and forerunner of the democratic league of Nations to come. Henceforth, we believe, because of this union, so natural yet so long delayed, by virtue of the ultimate victory it forecasts, the sun will never set on the Empire of the free, for the drum beats of democracy have been heard around the world. To this Empire will be added the precious culture of France, which the courage of her sons will have preserved, the contributions of Italy, and of Russia, yes, and of Japan.

Our philosophy and our religion are changing; hence it is more and more difficult to use the old terms to describe moral conduct. We say, for instance, that America's action in entering the war has been "unselfish." But this merely means that we have our own convictions concerning the ultimate comfort of the world, the manner of self-realization of individuals and nations. We are attempting to turn calamity into good. If this terrible conflict shall result in the inauguration of an emulative society, if it shall bring us to the recognition that intelligence and science may be used for the upbuilding of such an order, and for an eventual achievement of world peace, every sacrifice shall have been justified.

Such is the American Issue. Our statesmen and thinkers have helped to evolve it, our people with their blood and treasure are consecrating it. And these statesmen and thinkers, of whom our American President is not the least, are of democracy the pioneers. From the mountain tops on which they stand they behold the features of the new world, the dawn of the new day hidden as yet from their brothers in the valley. Let us have faith always that it is coming, and struggle on, highly resolving that those who gave their lives in the hour of darkness shall not have died in vain.

www.ingramcontent.com/pod-product-compliance
Lightning Source LLC
Chambersburg PA
CBHW022130280326
41933CB00007B/632